Shivi was amazed to see the clean city. There were beautiful paintings on the walls and the roads were lined with flowers.

So it is pretty and smart!

A Smart city tries to reduce traffic congestion and air pollution. It promotes open spaces with lots of trees, good road network and IT connectivity.

Nanu and Nani were delighted to see them but Tommy, their dog, was most excited. He kept jumping at Shivi and wagging his tail with happiness.

It was the turtle hatching season, so they got to see many tiny turtles being released into the water.

During the day, Shivi fed Tommy and gave him a bath. He became wet in the process!

How do you learn new words?
Try using them 5 times in the day.
Magic—the word belongs to you.

They stayed there the whole day and Shivi forgot about feeding Tommy.

"Let's go home now, it is time to feed Tommy."

The cable car connecting the Kailash hill park to the city is the first of its kind in Andhra Pradesh.

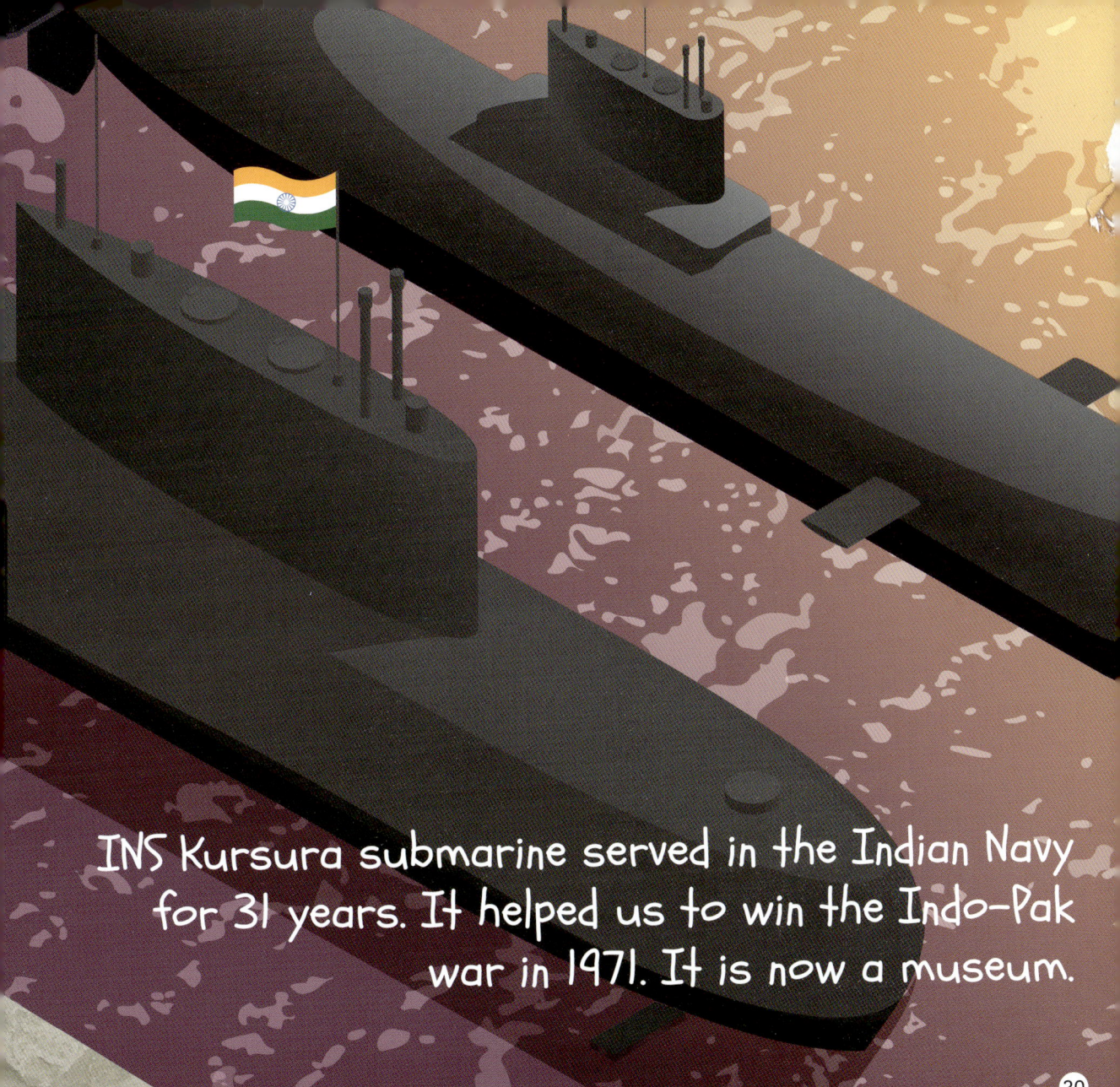

INS Kursura submarine served in the Indian Navy for 31 years. It helped us to win the Indo-Pak war in 1971. It is now a museum.

Next day Nanu, Mom and Shivi went to the zoo. Papa stayed home with Nani to learn how to make dosas.

There are 800 animals here!

Even the lions and tigers are not in cages!

When they got back, Shivi was excited about eating dosa but Papa just sat in front of the TV. Shivi started crying.

"You promised to make dosa for me. I'm so hungry!"

"I'm sure Tommy feels the same when you don't give him food on time."

The next day, they went to Borra caves which have stalactite and stalagmite formations.

Have you visited any UNESCO world heritage sites? Are there any in your city?

From there, they drove to Araku Valley for an overnight stay. Araku valley is famous for its coffee.

Araku is a small hill station like Ooty.

Papa, I remembered to bring Tommy's food. I have learnt res-pon-si-bi-lity.

By now, the holidays had come to an end, so, they all headed back home.

What do you enjoy most on your trips?

Date:

What do you enjoy most on your trips?

Date:

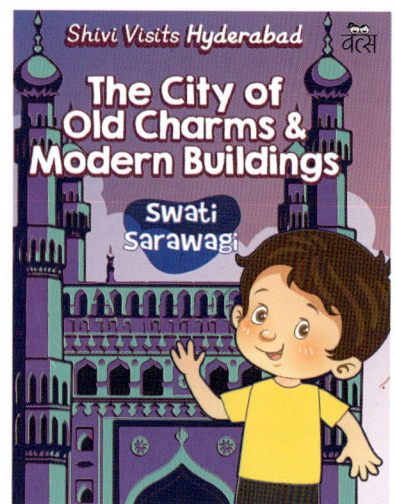
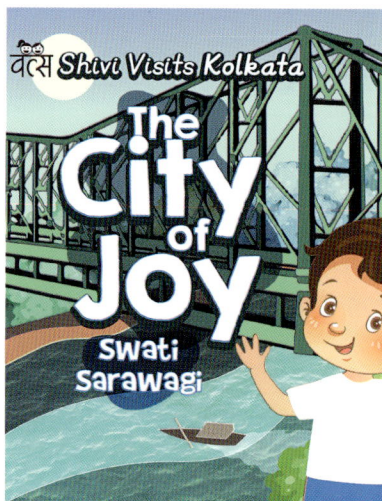
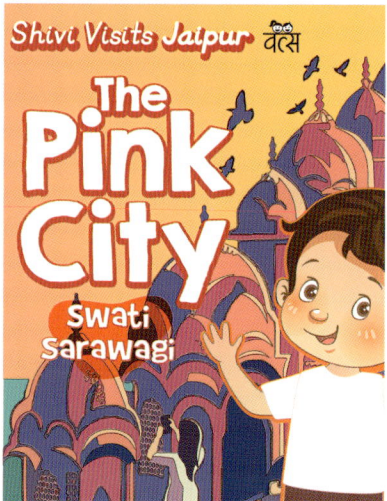